Fifteen Christmas Poems

and Some...

Johnny Coomansingh

*"And the angel came in unto her,
and said, hail, thou that art highly favored,
the Lord is with thee:
blessed art thou among women"*
(Luke 1:28)

Editor: Devanand Sooknanan, BA (Hons), History and
Literatures in English, University of the West Indies

Description for graphic on front cover: Sorrel (Hibiscus
sabdariffa) in bloom (Photo taken by author, 2015).

To order additional copies of this book, contact:
Xlibris
1-888-795-4274
www.Xlibris.com
Orders@Xlibris.com

ISBN: Softcover   978-1-7960-5912-0
         EBook   978-1-7960-5911-3

Print information available on the last page

Rev. date: 09/13/2019

Preface

Regardless of ethnicity, religious persuasion, creed, caste, class, or political opinions, I am sure that all of us believe that we could warm and make happy the hearts of others at Christmas. Reminiscent of the lines, "If I can help somebody as I pass along...if I can do my duty in a word or song, then my living shall not be in vain," it is my belief that true living begins when we contribute, when we share. Life is so much more meaningful when we foster acts of kindness to make someone else's life better and more meaningful; when the attitude of being a "Scrooge" departs. Christmastime allows the opportunity to negate the "scrooginess" in all of us. It's a time of deeper caring and sharing. It's a time of peace, love, and joy; yes, an exciting and exuberant moment in time; "It's the time of year when the world falls in love. Every song you hear seems to say: Merry Christmas, may your New Year dreams come true." When we cease to cherish such a moment we become "diseased" in mind, disoriented, confused, and miserable in spirit because we focus on ourselves more than others. Christmas is not about promoting unhappiness; it's not about "grinching" and "pinching." It's not a time of "lowness," not a time for stinginess; and certainly not a time for "tight hands." Explore the goodness that you possess in your soul! Release your blessings on all! Give more! Expect less! Christmas is about giving, not only at Christmastime, but giving with heart and soul all year through. Christmas culminates in the joy and gladness that we experienced during the course of the year, knowing that all year through we gave of our bounties, we shared and we cared about our "next door neighbor." I know of people who for years have never said "Hello" to the person living in the adjacent apartment. Even dogs and cats get along today. Let us not become cold and indifferent; share the warmth! Let us not become crass, callous, caustic and confrontational with those around us. Let us put on the mantle of love, peace, and joy...let's lift up Christ our Savior...the Christ in Christmas. "For unto us a child is born, unto us a son is given: and the government shall be upon his shoulder: and his name shall be called Wonderful, Counsellor, The Mighty God, The Everlasting Father, The Prince of Peace" (Isaiah 9:6).

Contents

"And I, if I be lifted up from the Earth, will draw all men unto me"
(John 12:32)

Glory to God in the highest...

"And it came to pass in those days, that there went out a decree from Caesar Augustus that all the world should be taxed. And this taxing was first made when Cyrenius was governor of Syria. And all went to be taxed, every one into his own city. And Joseph also went up from Galilee, out of the city of Nazareth, into Judaea, unto the city of David, which is called Bethlehem; because he was of the house and lineage of David: To be taxed with Mary his espoused wife, being great with child. And so it was, that, while they were there, the days were accomplished that she should be delivered. And she brought forth her firstborn son, and wrapped him in swaddling clothes, and laid him in a manger; because there was no room for them in the inn. And there were in the same country shepherds abiding in the field, keeping watch over their flock by night. And, lo, the angel of the Lord came upon them, and the glory of the Lord shone round about them: and they were sore afraid. And the angel said unto them, Fear not: for, behold, I bring you good tidings of great joy, which shall be to all people. For unto you is born this day in the city of David a Savior, which is Christ the Lord. And this shall be a sign unto you; Ye shall find the babe wrapped in swaddling clothes, lying in a manger. And suddenly there was with the angel a multitude of the heavenly host praising God, and saying, Glory to God in the highest, and on earth peace, good will toward men" (Luke 2: 1-14)

There is "Light & Truth" for all...

I am convinced that we will overcome our deepest fears when we cease to subscribe to dogma, ritual, and liturgy. With an open and fertile mind, we must allow for the revelation of truth in its glorious simplicity...to sift and winnow away illusions and accept the reality of the moment. No one needs anyone to unravel or decipher the "mystery" about truth, for truth in itself is not mysterious...no, not at all mysterious (Coomansingh, 2003).

Let Christmas Be (2003)

Let Christmas be every day of the year,
Let Christmas be smiling children without a tear,
Let Christmas be tables full of joy,
Enough for every girl and every boy.

Let Christmas be a moment in my heart,
Of peace, of love, of joy right from the start,
Let Christmas be the feeling to be with friends,
Let Christmas be the carols when our voices blend.

Let Christmas be the story of our Lord and Christ,
Who became the ultimate sacrifice,
Born in a manger…and yes,
To his own people a stranger.

Let Christmas be the time to care and share,
Let Christmas be the time to offer a prayer,
For those who fight for our freedom,
With the hope for peace in an everlasting kingdom.

Let Christmas be the season to purge the hate,
From our souls…offer to God a clean slate,
Where the Spirit could write the law of love,
Emerge as a new receptacle filled from above.

Let Christmas be freedom from hagglers,
Bartering goods to the hurried and the stragglers,
Let Christmas be richer…a time to store,
Good deeds of faith…an open eye towards the poor.

Let Christmas be a time for humankind,
To rest the weary, tired mind,
To ponder on the blessings of life so free,
It is high time to let Christmas be!

From Sangre Grande tuh Pinto Road…in ah Parang (2004)

Ah scratchin' mih head, buh ah cyar remember the year
Buh with dat yuh have tuh bear
Anyhow, ah remember the time
Dem fellas from WASA take mih for a Parang lime.

It was ah Christmas Eve night
Ah put mih head on mih pillow and switch off mih light
Then ah hear ah cuatro, ah box base, and ah marac
Ah wasn't dreaming so ah roll over on mih back.

One o'clock in the morning dem fellas come
Lavway in the corridor with ah glorious song
I eh have no choice, ah had tuh rub mih eye
Tuh play ah cuatro ah didn't have tuh try.

Sweet, sweet parang in a narrow corridor
Sweet, sweet Aguinaldo jus' outside mih door

Ah throw on some clothes and ah invite them in
Ah take up mih cuatro and ah start tuh sing.

We sing ah lavway by Ava mih sister, and cousin Larry
Valencia was the next stop tuh make people merry
One parandero had a nasty tabanca…
Crying for no reason while shaking the maracas.

He say he gyul lef him for nutten at all
Then he start tuh pong he hand against the wall
Buh the fellas tell him doh mind dat
She go come back tuh yuh like ah stray way cat.

He felt ah lil better although he buss up he hand
It was Christmas time, parang, rejoicing across the land
We end up in Pinto Road in a squatter settlement
And brought the joy of Christmas the Savior sent.

The love in Pinto Road among the simple and poor
Was more than enough as we "serenaled" from door to door
The smell of new linoleum…the smiles, I will never forget
They were some of the happiest people I have ever met.

Yes, from Grande tuh Pinto Road tuh spread the love
Related in the Parang about the Peace from above
So many people made happy on dat Christmas Day
Today and forever, let the sweet Parang play.

Chorus of a parang song we sang at Pinto Road

Coro, coro, coro, coro celestial,
El hijo de Maria, viene adorar.

Los pastores diquen, vieron bajar,
Una luz del cielo, derecho portal.

Sereno, sereno, a vendio,
Vamos a gozar, Con gran alegria!

Maria lloraba, Maria lloro
LLoro por su nino, cuando los perdio.

Alegria! alegria!
Alegria, en mi corazon!

> *"Bless the Lord, O my soul: and all that is within me, bless his holy name."*
> (Psalm 103: 1)

Figure 1. Sometimes a band of paranderos might come upon a house that looks foreboding, dark and unapproachable like this one in the photograph. At times, they have to beat down and trample the overgrowth to get to the door. Nevertheless, good paranderos will strive to make people happy and joyous with a good parang! There is nothing in this world that will deter their purpose in bringing merriment and gladness to a home at Christmas (Photograph by author)

Parang...a synopsis

Celebrated in Trinidad and Tobago from as early as September 25th, the Parang (parranda) embraces the Christmas spirit with song, dance, food, and music. Several instruments facilitate the Parang including the cuatro (the lead instrument), the maracas (shac-shac), mandolin, scratchers, box base, guitar, and sometimes a violin. To keep the pace (beat) and rhythm, two cylindrical pieces of solid wood, about one inch in diameter, six to eight inches long, are knocked together. These are known as "tock-tocks." Christmas without parang in Trinidad is like carnival in Trinidad without steelpan and calypso.

With the Parang comes the "smell" of Christmas emanating from the food. Baked ham, pastelles, black (fruit) cake, coconut sweetbread, homemade bread, cassava pone, sorrel drink, ponche de crème, and ginger beer. These are some of the items that come to mind for consumption at Christmas. Parang takes the paranderos on long carefree journeys making music, "serenaling" from house to house, at least when I was a boy.

Figure 2. A pair of maracas (shac-shacs) and a pair of tock-tocks. With a handle attached, the maracas are normally made from calabash (*Crescentia cujete*) gourds (Photograph by author)

The poem, "From Grande to Pinto Road" is about my personal Parang experience. Several young men, most of them employed with the Water And Sewerage Authority (WASA) "boarded" my apartment on Christmas at 1:00 am. I was just about to retire to bed having traveled from Salmady Village, Tamana where I left my family. I was supposed to spend Christmas day at my in-laws, but that was not to be. I remembered that we did not close the bedroom windows before we left for Tamana. Since Sangre Grande has earned the moniker as the "Bathroom of Trinidad," I hastened to have them shut. I shut the windows but I had no shut eye after that. A drenched apartment would have surely dampened spirits.

As I was about to take my first nod into slumber land, there arose this "sweet" noise wafting on the air in the corridor in front of my door. I thought I was dreaming but no, it was ah real Trini Parang right outside. I woke as though in a dream and asked myself, "could this be ah real Parang?" I did not hear a sound, not even a shuffle, as the paranderos gathered in the corridor. The music struck up and it was not my imagination. The sound of a box base, shac-shac, guitar and cuatro blended together as the men started ah "lavway." It was Parang in front mih door! The poem: "From Sangre Grande to Pinto Road" says it all…

The "Cocoa Panyols" and Parang

"It is almost certain that the *Cocoa Panyols* (estate laborers) from Venezuela introduced the Parranda to Trinidad. The mention of Parang necessitates an explanation of what comprises this musical and festive activity. Parang as part of our heritage, our culture, is basically associated with feting and merrymaking at Christmastime. Small groups of villagers comprising about four or five men, the *paranderos*, would sometimes engage in an *aparrandaat* at festive events, for example, a baby's christening or a person's birthday. Singing Spanish ballads at such celebrations accompanied with musical instruments gave rise to a jovial atmosphere; pure merriment. Such instruments included the *cuatro* (small four-stringed instrument derived from the Portuguese *cavaquinho*), guitar, bandolin, tok-tok, a salt box base, a pair of *maracas* or *shac-shac* and maybe a fiddle and a mandolin. The cuatro is considered to be the national instrument of Venezuela. There are claims that the Parang practiced in Trinidad and Tobago today came from Venezuela, in the form known as *parranda navidena* or "Christmas parang."

With just seven miles east across the Gulf of Paria, the relative location of Trinidad to Venezuela probably encouraged the acceptance and growth of Parang with all its folkloric trappings into Trinidad. It is clear, because of proximity, that cultural exchanges were attributable to the constant interaction between the island and the South American mainland. Around Christmastime, the Parang musical art-form envelops the landscape. Who brought the Parang is still uncertain. Was it the "cocoa panyols" or the Spanish colonists (1498-1797)? No one can really give an exact and conclusive answer as to who brought the Parang. Nevertheless, Parang is now widespread on the cultural landscape of Trinidad.

Citing a snippet of an article produced by the Trinidad and Tobago National Library (*www.nalis. gov.tt*) "...Parang has been called a fusion of the deep spiritual aspirations of the Spanish people and the unfettered joyfulness of the Amerindian and African cultures." Regardless of its origins, style, instruments, people, songs, and performance format, Parang found its way among the estate workers, for example, in Sangre Grande, Sangre Chiquito, Rio Claro, Tamana, Palo Seco, and in most localities where entrepreneurs produced cocoa in Trinidad. Moreover, Parang has always been an activity flavored with singing, merriment, dancing, instrumentalists, and obviously, the preparation and sharing of special food and drink.

Figure 3. A beautiful pair of cocoa pods. This photo was taken along the road to Biche village, Trinidad. (Photograph by author)

Nevertheless, all good things must come to an end. The melodious tones of men and women in an exultant and sweet Parang wafting on the rural midnight air among the cocoa estate workers gradually came to a hush. Many of the estate barracks on plantations where workers lived were soon vacated. There was trouble on the international cocoa market. Without a means of earning a daily wage, laborers left. As with every commodity on the world market, supply and demand affect prices...people, and folkways." (Adapted from the book: "Cocoa Woman" by Johnny Coomansingh).

A parang joke

About dusk dark, late one Christmas evening, two old payols decided to go on a parang lime in the village not too far away. Their home was separated by a little dirt track with a few overhanging shrubs such as blacksage, wild guava, and keskidee, which from time-to-time were cleanly cut back with a poinyah (machete) leaving some pretty sharp ends on the branches. One of the men was totally blind while the other was one-eyed. The blind man was the cuatro player. The one-eyed man was the guide. Dey say ah one-eye man is king in blind man country, and this was fact right here! So it happened that the two of them started on their little trek to the village. The funny thing was that every now and then the blind cuatro man would stop and start tuh lavway ah tune with the cuatro. The one-eye compai would turn around and say to him: "Not yet compai. Not yet. When we reach whe we going ah will tell yuh tuh play." Ah go say "We reach!" This happened quite a few times until the low pointed end of a branch juk (pricked) the one-eye man inside he good eye. He screamed in pain while saying: "Compai we reach whe we going!" Guess what happened in the track after he said those words.

A little story about my cuatro named "Sonah"

Figure 4. A parandero and his cuatro…friends forever! (Photograph by Josh Branche)

Here I am, toting my made in Venezuela, "El Torrense" cuatro. In 2003, my cousin, Trevor, bought this cuatro from *Simon Music Supplies*, in Trinidad. For whatever reason, I immediately named it "Sonah," even though I had no clue what the word *Sonah* meant. Long after, I found out that "sona" meant "gold." In Hindi, "sona" means gold; very pretty; lovely; sweet; heat; fiery. I etched on it "Sonah" because of the gallant tones this instrument emits. The "action" on this box is exceptional! What a voice! Such crispness and clarity!

On my journeys abroad and thinking about how to "advertise" Trinidad and Tobago, I painted the colors of the national flag on the slap board, but due to wear, I removed the paint and overlaid the slap board with a piece Trinidad grown teak wood less than one-thirty second of an inch thick. Doused with a little olive oil, the teak I reasoned, will not wear as fast as the cedar wood. With the refurbished slap board, the instrument developed a certain sweetness of tone, unsurpassed. It "stings!" This cuatro has been my friend in many a soire...when there was need for accompaniment, hymns, choruses, calypso (kaiso), folk songs, and most of all, Parang. I used this cuatro as my prime instrument for accompaniment when I recorded in Trini dialect, the Soca-Parang song below. Here are a few lines:

"The Road Have ah Hole in Valencia:"
Ah was going up tuh Grande fuh di Christmas
Ah was going up tuh Grande fuh di Christmas
Ah end up in ah hole
On di Valencia Stretch
Ah end up in ah hole
Ah cannot find di depth.

<u>Chorus.</u>
Di road have ah hole in Valencia
Di road have ah hole in Valencia
How dat hole come dey
Nobody cannot say
How dat hole come dey
Nobody cannot say.

It was trouble in the hole for di Christmas
It was trouble in the hole for di Christmas
Ah did have ah plan
Tuh make a good Parang
Ah did have ah plan
Tuh make a good Parang...

Mih cuatro come and buss in the hole
Mih cuatro come and buss in the hole
Mih axle come and break
No more ah cannot take
Mih axle come and break
No more ah cannot take...

Then people laff at mih on di roadside
Then people laff at mih on di roadside
I is ah choopidee
For falling in di hole
I is ah choopidee
For falling in di hole.

...for out of thee shall come a Governor

"Now when Jesus was born in Bethlehem of Judaea in the days of Herod the king, behold, there came wise men from the east to Jerusalem, Saying, Where is he that is born King of the Jews? for we have seen his star in the east, and are come to worship him. When Herod the king had heard *these things*, he was troubled, and all Jerusalem with him. And when he had gathered all the chief priests and scribes of the people together, he demanded of them where Christ should be born. And they said unto him, In Bethlehem of Judaea: for thus it is written by the prophet…And thou Bethlehem, *in* the land of Juda, art not the least among the princes of Juda: for out of thee shall come a Governor, that shall rule my people Israel. Then Herod, when he had privily called the wise men, inquired of them diligently what time the star appeared. And he sent them to Bethlehem, and said, Go and search diligently for the young child; and when ye have found *him*, bring me word again, that I may come and worship him also. When they had heard the king, they departed; and, lo, the star, which they saw in the east, went before them, till it came and stood over where the young child was. When they saw the star, they rejoiced with exceeding great joy. And when they were come into the house, they saw the young child with Mary his mother, and fell down, and worshipped him: and when they had opened their treasures, they presented unto him gifts; gold, and frankincense, and myrrh. And being warned of God in a dream that they should not return to Herod, they departed into their own country another way. And when they were departed, behold, the angel of the Lord appeareth to Joseph in a dream, saying, Arise, and take the young child and his mother, and flee into Egypt, and be thou there until I bring thee word: for Herod will seek the young child to destroy him. When he arose, he took the young child and his mother by night, and departed into Egypt: And was there until the death of Herod: that it might be fulfilled which was spoken of the Lord by the prophet, saying, out of Egypt have I called my son" (Matthew 2: 1-15).

The Christmas Angel (2005)

The angel said unto me, "write!"
Write! write! write! about this dreadful night
And the people who seek to make the season bright,
By hanging on a cone-bearing tree a million lights.

Write about the folks who traverse the land
With a shopping list glued to their hand,
To find the very last gift

The hope of giving someone a pleasant lift.
But as the angel said
Clear thy head…
Carry a new message—not of reindeer, not of Santa
Celebrate Christ, the blessed Savior!

The angel continued: "Who is this Jack Frost?"
He has become more than a mafia boss,
Constantly nipping at purse and nose
And leaves us altogether so comatose.

For many "righteous" churchgoers
Are just plain talkers—no doers,
Simplicity they forever negate
Self-righteousness and pomp they celebrate.

Write! I say unto thee
About the people, who all year long lack love and mercy,
Yes, those who forget the stinking, smelly stable!
And a child lying in a straw-lined cradle.

"Don't stop now," the angel said, "Write some more"
About a Man, tired, sorrowful—The Door,
Who waits with open arms to welcome the poor
At Christmas, and every day of the year to adore.

Write about His suffering, His tears, His pain
Bleeding, dying on a cross of sin and shame,
For those lost in the mall, the giant maze,
In a world where right and wrong are locked in a nasty haze.

Ah Real Trini Christmas (2006)

All year long ah paying Chin for mih ham
Look at mih crosses; I eh have no pitch-oil pan,
Livin' in tong, ah cyar put mih hand on three big stone
Confusion, comesse, ah cyar call mih tantie…dey cut mih phone.

So ah decide to spend Christmas in Sangre Grande
Up dey have plenty sorrel, and plenty rock and mauby,
Sweetest Parang, sweetbread, black cake, pastelle and souse
Yes believe mih…yuh could go and eat in anybody house.

So ah tote mih ham and ah dress up in mih Sunday best tay-lay-lay
Ah have tuh make it tuh Grande by Christmas Eve day,
To drink a ponche de crème on Christmas Eve night
Nothing better than dat…with ah lil Angostura, yuh mus get it right.

Campo and dem fellas planning tuh buss mih bar
Dey coming from Manzan, Vega, Tamana…from near and far,
Ah shine up mih cuatro, ah gih it some dew and tighten the string
All ah waiting to do now is Parang…ah have ah lavway tuh sing.

When ah reach Cunapo on Christmas Eve day
People busy, busy, busy, so ah get outa dey way,

Some still shopping…Trincity, Gulf City Mall…oui foote, mamayo
Some ah dem woman still looking for ripe horse plantain from Toco.

Dey now painting the step?…oh mih lard!
What? Dey still cleaning the yard?
Some drilling hole tuh hang up curtain
Some go lose dey mind today…dat is for certain.

So Christmas come, and Christmas gone
Everybody tired…dey leggo, leggo, lying dong,
Ah tell mihself…homemade bread, sorrel, and ah slice ah ham
Ah go eat and drink an' then ah go jam.

Leh dem sleep…leh dem sprawl out on dey precious polish floor,
You think I worrying 'bout dat…breda close the door,
Ah gone back tuh Port of Spain tuh see the lights
On the Brian Lara Promenade it rel nice on Christmas night.

Mih family eat dong mih ham…buh ah have the bone
On Boxing Day the soup is mine, and mine alone,
An' when the Soca start tuh blast…yuh have tuh get in gear
Carnaval 'round di corner, jus' after we celebrate the New Year.

Christmas in Trinidad

I take it upon myself to accept any "blows," backchat, or criticisms, destructive or otherwise, from anyone concerning my "biased" view that "Trini Christmas is di best!" I don't think that there's any place in the whole wide world that could boast of celebrating a better Christmastime than the people of Trinidad….hmmm, not even in Israel. I cannot say much about Tobago because I have never celebrated Christmas on the sister isle. I will assume that they will share the same views as mine. A few snippets of our traditions will follow to allow a better understanding this Christmas thing we Trinis love so much.

The "Ham and the Pitch-oil pan tradition" in Trinidad and Tobago is an aspect of the Trini Christmas that is worth sharing. In this little, English-speaking, democratic, republic, Christmas is a very, very special occasion. Preparations to welcome Christmas Day begin many months before the actual Christmas season. In fact, the annual Parang (parranda), a musical festival that heralds the onset of the Christmas season begins on September 25th. The Parang is one thing, but what would Parang be without a Christmas ham? Extremely important is the presentation of a well-decorated ham on Christmas Day.

Figure 5. "The Shell Angel," constructed out of seashells collected from a Florida beach. I made this Christmas tree ornament and shipped it to my friends in a place called Bachus, Minnesota (Photograph by author)

During my childhood, shops and grocers, at least in Sangre Grande and suburbs, carried the famous Picnic hams that someone said came from Canada. These hams, packaged in tar paper and cotton bags were normally strung up for viewing by customers on a thick wire that stretched from one side of the grocery to the other. Customers would sometimes make a down payment on a ham many months before Christmas Day. Their names were also inscribed on the chosen ham and everyone knew what ham belonged to whom. In some cases, customers paid monthly or weekly installments on their hams until the full amount was paid. Invariably, ham owners would pay off the bill and collect their hams by Christmas Eve day.

Traditionally, hams were boiled in the yard of the household in a four or five-gallon container (pan) made of tin. This pan normally contained bulk cooking oil and came to be known as a "pitch-oil" pan because villagers would convert the empty cans to carry pitch oil (kerosene). The pitch-oil pan is probably the size of the present-day large *Crix* biscuit container. Pitch-oil pans are hardly seen around today, and for the most part, extinct. To boil the ham, a wood fire would be lit between three large stones. The pitch-oil pan with the ham would be placed on the three stones and allowed to boil, sometimes for the greater part of Christmas Eve day. After the boiling process, the ham was sometimes baked and decorated with cloves, pineapple and red cherries. Never is anything better than homemade bread and a slice of ham on a Christmas morning garnished with "Chow-Chow," the famous *Larjochow* pepper sauce, ketchup, and a leaf of lettuce. Everybody in our house looked forward to this once-a-year treat served with hot creole chocolate "tea." The homemade chocolate balls were grated and boiled with cinnamon and a leaf or two of bayleaf. Whole milk or evaporated milk and condensed milk were added to the boiled chocolate to complete the beverage. As someone said: "Yuh could see the grease from the cocoa floating on top."

Black cake (fruit/rum cake), "Christmas" biscuits, wafers, dates, grapes, apples, almonds, hazelnuts, Brazil nuts, walnuts, cashew nuts, and prunes were part of the Christmas fare. We saw such items only at Christmastime. My mother would also bake a couple loaves of coconut sweetbread. Consisting of baked chicken, potato salad with hard-boiled eggs, beetroot, boiled plantains, fresh watercress, callaloo, and fried rice, our Christmas lunch was always special. On most occasions, the Christmas tree was just a guava or black sage branch covered with cotton to represent snow. An old bucket or paint can filled with sand and rocks would be used to accommodate the branch. The container would normally be covered over with Christmas wrapping paper. The itchy and scratchy "angel hair" made of fiberglass was also used as part of the decoration. The bright red, green, blue, and yellow bulbs on the tree brought with them a certain feeling…a Christmas feeling. As far as Christmas drinks were concerned, homemade sorrel and ginger beer were always on the list. Of course there would also be a couple bottles of Old Oak rum, cherry brandy, Charlie's red wine, and some soft drinks in the cupboard.

"Make a joyful noise unto the Lord. all ye lands. Serve the Lord with gladness…"
(Psalm 100: 1-2)

A brief note about Sorrel (*Hibiscus sabdariffa*)

It is difficult to ascertain who brought the sorrel plant to the shores of my homeland, Trinidad and Tobago. Nevertheless, it is believed that sorrel came from West Africa with enslaved Africans who involuntarily arrived on these shores after the grueling journey through the *Middle Passage*. Sorrel has many uses. Especially during the Yuletide season, sorrel is used in the creation of a bright red Christmas drink.

There are other varieties of sorrel, including the white type, a very dark red, and one with a an almost black inflorescence. The more common type, with a red floral calyx in the mature stage, is brewed to extract the red astringent drink. The drink is then sweetened and served over cracked ice.

Sorrel could be used also to make healthful hot tea, sorrel liqueur, wines, dressing for turkey as a substitute for cranberry sauce, sorrel jam, daquiris, and cordials. Most West Indian (Caribbean) stores in the United States sell dried sorrel. Here's a recipe for making sorrel drink:

Recipe for making sorrel drink

Ingredients	Method
10 quarts water	Bring water to a boil with cloves and cinnamon
454 grams (1 lb) dried sorrel flowers	Place sorrel in boiling water and turn off stove
12-15 cloves	Allow sorrel to steep overnight
4 large sticks of cinnamon	Strain liquid through a cheese cloth
Sugar (brown or white)	Sweeten to taste with sugar
	Add one cup cherry brandy in the mix.
	Serve over cracked ice

Figure 6 . Sorrel inflorescence (Photograph by author)

If We Could Only...(2007)

If we could only learn our bounties to share,
If we could only have the will to care,
If we could only flash a genuine smile,
If we could only "walk the second mile."

If we could only foster true friendship,
If we could only ease the "sting" of the whip,
If we could only bridle the wayward tongue,
If we could only remove the silly frown.

If we could only forget the horror of the past,
If we could only make a sweet moment last,
If we could only "stay on our knees" a minute longer,
If we could only help someone to be a little stronger.

If we could only with love, light a Christmas tree,
If we could only say there is no malice in me,
If we could only take the hand of a sister, a brother,
If we could only be at peace with each other.

If we could only know how to stop a hellish war,
If we could only find the true and living door,
If we could only tread the straight and narrow road,
If we could only help with each other's load.
If We Could Only Love…

Figure 7. There is something really special about Christmas; something that moves the heart and touches the soul. Yes, something that brings out the humanity in all of us. The music, the love, the joy, the peace and good tidings…that's something special! (Photograph by Carlyle Horrell)

… *and shalt call his name* Jesus

And the angel said unto her, Fear not, Mary: for thou hast found favor with God. And, behold, thou shalt conceive in thy womb, and bring forth a son, and shalt call his name JESUS. He shall be great, and shall be called the Son of the Highest: and the Lord God shall give unto him the throne of his father David: And he shall reign over the house of Jacob forever; and of his kingdom there shall be no end (Luke 1:30-33).

Christmas lights…(2008)

Everywhere I look, I see the lights,
Lights of Christmas to brighten the night;
The night of hopelessness, fear,
Big corporations do not care!

Yet, we buy their lights by the bundle,
Nobody hears the economic rumble,
House foreclosures, people bawl and wail,
While heartless companies ask for a money bail.

By rail, by truck, by car, to Washington we go,
Leave corporate jets behind, the Feds must never know
That we eat caviar and drink champagne,
Keep the poor man on a money strain.

And the little man, the paltry little man,
Could never understand the horrible plan,
How one man, in one year, makes $21 million,
While he for gas, pays four dollars a gallon.

Teary-eyed, he hopes for the Christmas lights,
Broken, he struggles with all his might,
To clothe and feed his little girls and boys…
Fill their stocking with *plastic* toys.

And somewhere on a track in my mind,
One rode on a donkey so gentle and kind,
The King of Lights…yes, of peace and joy,
Mary's precious little baby boy.

The *Child of Light* is what we all need,
Truth and sincerity not mingled with greed,
Seek Him; find Him, ye of Abraham's seed,
'Twas for you, He, in sorrow did bleed.
…find and share that Light.

Ye are the light of the world. A city that is set on an hill cannot be hid. Neither do men light a candle, and put it under a bushel, but on a candlestick; and it giveth light unto all...
(Matthew 5: 14-16)

Figure 8. The glorious and beautiful blooms of the Petrea plant (*Petrea volubillis*) serves to adorn the surroundings of the all wooden Morton Memorial Presbyterian Church in Guaico, Sangre Grande. Dr. John Morton, a minister of the Presbyterian Church of Nova Scotia, Canada, established this church in 1898. This church is testament to the courage and fortitude of Presbyterian pioneers and missionaries who came to Trinidad. William Hugh Benjamin from Scotland who had a bakery in Guaico assisted Dr. John Morton, with the lumber to erect the Morton Memorial Presbyterian Church and the Guaico Presbyterian Primary School. The pews, constructed of roughhewn local lumber, are still present and in use in this church to this day. The church, now part of the National Trust of Trinidad and Tobago, was granted the award for being the best kept small historical building in the country. I love this photograph, and I thought it nice to share it with everyone (Photograph by author)

Go Back to the Stable *(2009)*

Born in a stable?
A manger for a cradle?
A bed of straw?
So humble and so poor?
Toiling at the carpenter's table?
Many today treat as a fable?
Bearing my burden?
So downtrodden?
Forgiving every time?
He the Mount of Olives climbed?
No bed? No pillow for His head?

He made the blind man see?
And supplicated for you and me?
Giving bread to the hungry?
Trudging the road to Calvary?
Speaking the sweet and sincere word?
Fought not with sticks and sword?
Taking my sorrow?
Promising a brighter tomorrow?
I know you know the answer for every question,
I know the struggle for your tongue to mention,
I know that you are busy with the familiar institution,
I know of the preparation for the Christmas tradition.
Forget the mall! Go back to the stable!
Dig, search; find the recipe to be humble,
Turn around! Go back to the place!
See the peace, the glory in your Savior's face.
He came for you…Do you know His voice?
He will sup with you…Is it your choice?
It was all about *you* from the very beginning,
Come, rest; sip from His blessed fountain.

Let us now go into Bethlehem…

"And it came to pass, as the angels were gone away from them into heaven, the shepherds said one to another, Let us now go even unto Bethlehem, and see this thing which is come to pass, which the Lord hath made known unto us. And they came with haste, and found Mary, and Joseph, and the babe lying in a manger. And when they had seen it, they made known abroad the saying which was told them concerning this child. And all they that heard it wondered at those things which were told them by the shepherds. But Mary kept all these things, and pondered them in her heart. And the shepherds returned, glorifying and praising God for all the things that they had heard and seen, as it was told unto them. And when eight days were accomplished for the circumcising of the child, his name was called JESUS, which was so named of the angel before he was conceived in the womb. And when the days of her purification according to the law of Moses were accomplished, they brought him to Jerusalem, to present him to the Lord; (As it is written in the law of the LORD, Every male that openeth the womb shall be called holy to the Lord;) And to offer a sacrifice according to that which is said in the law of the Lord, A pair of turtledoves, or two young pigeons. And, behold, there was a man in Jerusalem, whose name was Simeon; and the same man was just and devout, waiting for the consolation of Israel: and the Holy Ghost was upon him. And it was revealed unto him by the Holy Ghost, that he should not see death, before he had seen the Lord's Christ" (Luke 2: 15-26)

"…for mine eyes have seen thy salvation"

"And he came by the Spirit into the temple: and when the parents brought in the child Jesus, to do for him after the custom of the law, then took he him up in his arms, and blessed God, and said, Lord, now lettest thou thy servant depart in peace, according to thy word: For mine eyes have seen thy salvation, which thou hast prepared before the face of all people; a light to lighten the Gentiles, and the glory of

thy people Israel. And Joseph and his mother marveled at those things which were spoken of him. And Simeon blessed them, and said unto Mary his mother, behold, this child is set for the fall and rising again of many in Israel; and for a sign which shall be spoken against; yea, a sword shall pierce through thy own soul also,) that the thoughts of many hearts may be revealed. And there was one Anna, a prophetess, the daughter of Phanuel, of the tribe of Aser: she was of a great age, and had lived with an husband seven years from her virginity; and she was a widow of about fourscore and four years, which departed not from the temple, but served God with fastings and prayers night and day. And she coming in that instant gave thanks likewise unto the Lord, and spake of him to all them that looked for redemption in Jerusalem. And when they had performed all things according to the law of the Lord, they returned into Galilee, to their own city Nazareth. And the child grew, and waxed strong in spirit, filled with wisdom: and the grace of God was upon him"
(Luke 2: 27-40).

Behold the Child of Joy (2010)
To the City of David, come…
Come with me to Bethlehem
Come with me to the stable
Come, be quiet in your soul
Come, see the Savior of the world
Lying wrapped in swaddling clothes.
Come, see the precious little baby
Some say that "He Come from the Glory"
Some say that He came to fulfill the story
That man will live forever more!
Come, taste of the water of life…
Come, forget the worry and the strife.
"Come see a man" she said
Come, with the Bread of Life be fed
Slowly walk, humbly kneel
It's the Savior…He is what's real
Feel His power in your heart
Let Him comfort you, just yield.
Come, find youself in the quiet place
Come, and look into His face
Touch Him, hold Him
Know His tenderness from within
And we know His future what it will be
To carry for us a cross to Calvary.
Give up your ramblings and rage
Gaze upon His visage…just gaze
Let Him heal…make you smile
For the first and every other mile
It's Christmas because ofMary's boy
Come, behold the Child of Joy!

Figure 9. This beautiful picture was photographed from a painting that was resurrected from the basement of the Foxholm Roman Catholic Church in North Dakota. No one in the parish knows its history, how it came to be lodged at the church. This wonderful and unique painting has since been restored and is now hanging in the foyer of the church. (Used with permission of the Abbey of Maria Laach, Germany)

Figure 10. Split Rock Lighthouse on the north shore of Lake Superior, Duluth, Minnesota (Photograph by author)

The Lighthouse (2011)

Upon a rock
One chilly day
I gazed amidst
The misty haze
At a lighthouse
Firmly built.

In its magnificence
It stood so proud
Above the lake
Through storm and cloud
For many a ship
A beacon of salvation.

Penetrating the mists
In the years gone by
Hope and gladness
For a sailor's eye
Now lightless in its beauty
A place defunct.

And then to an era past
I jog my mind
And inside therein
A lighthouse find
Still reaching out
With beams so bright.

If we all could go back
To the lighthouse there
To lend a hand,
A ray of hope with others share
At Christmas
And every day.

For Jesus is the lighthouse
Built upon the rock
That shines forever
To clear away the mire,
The muck
Of hate and scorn among the flock.

Begin today
To let your lighthouse shine
Don't wait for Christmas
As the only time
For in the mists
There are sailors and ships.

Is it so difficult? (2012)

To walk a weary road
To help with another's load
Is it so difficult?
To accept a humble stable
To see a straw-lined cradle
Is it so difficult?
To be born in a manger
To come to his own and treated as a stranger
Is it so difficult?
To walk the second mile
To be slapped, and still smile
Is it so difficult?
To acknowledge the poor
To welcome the homeless at your door
Is it so difficult?

To accept loss
To bear the cross
Is it so difficult?
To love your friends, your buddies
To love as well your enemies
Is it so difficult?
To stay the utter of the hateful word
To know "vengeance is mine," thus saith the Lord
Is it so difficult?
To live without fear or favor
To simply love your neighbor

Figure 11. Christmas cheer on steelpan, the national instrument of Trinidad and Tobago, at the Trincity Mall, Trinidad
(Photograph by author)

Is it so difficult?
To right all wrongs
To sing a lifting song
Is it so difficult?
To walk the thorny path
To give with a cheerful heart
Is it so difficult?
To see your reflection in your Savior's face
To experience only His saving grace
Is it so difficult?

Figure 12. A decorated piece of driftwood I collected from the Grande Riviere beach, Trinidad. I enjoyed carving this piece picked from the rocks. It is now part of the Christmas décor in the sitting room of an American home (Photograph by author)

"...and they shall call his name Emmanuel,
which being interpreted is, God with us.
(Matthew 1:23)

'Tis Shining Still (2013)

The Star of Bethlehem
Followed by three wise men,
To a stable…
And a straw-lined cradle.

Adorned by the glorious light
To shine, to dispel a sinful night,
The world at the end of its rope,
Receives a gift; new hope.

For in that crude little cradle
In that putrid, smelly stable,
Was my Savior, my wonderful Lord,
The divine and Living Word.

He grew, He preached, He witnessed
My example, my joy, my righteousness,

And yet endured the shame; a cruel cross,
For you, for me; for all of us.

At least at Christmas do take a look
Riffle the pages of the good old book,
For in every one of us there is a need,
Heal your soul; read!

And the peace He bestows
Shields us "From every stormy wind that blows,"
For His yoke is easy and His burden light,
Come and be blest; make it right.

So humble, so helpless, so poor He came
Yield, adore; praise His holy name
Rejoice! Give to Him your heart, your will,
The glorious Star, 'tis shining still.

"Glory to God in the highest, and on earth peace, good will toward men"
(Luke 2:14)

Christmas in Divers Places (2014)

So it's Christmas in Texas, yippee!
Peace and goodwill to everybody!
Carols and the feeling of cheer…O dear,
Looking forward to a happy New Year?
It's also Christmas in Mississippi,
O come let us all sing lustily
"Angels we have heard on high," hallelujah!
And "We three kings of orient are."

Yep…it's Christmas in North Dakota,
Where live the Mandan, Hidatsa, and Arikara,
Those Native Americans, who for the life of me
Still hope for a better Christmas story.

It's Christmas in New York,
Where there is talk, talk, talk,
Great city of lights, business and money
Let's go see that big Christmas tree.

Now let's look at Christmas in Missouri,
Look at Christmas in *Ferguson*, let's see
A burnt out city…crying for its dead,
Hmmm, a young man pumped full of lead.

And he is gone, like God's only son;
Gone, gone, gone; a mother's child, gone!
He bled, he died…
And we cried.

It's Christmas in Washington,
Where seat warming is an institution,
Here they savor procrastination,
Thumb-twiddling is now a noble occupation.

And despite the Christmas cheer, and all that holly,
For the coming year let's continue the folly
Of hating one another,
Don't you get it…what's your race, your color?

It's Christmas, we go to church; we pray
For a better day…O God! We need a better way!
Surely, we all must pass through the gate…
Wait! Leave it outside, the hate.

With his stripes…

"Who hath believed our report? And to whom is the arm of the LORD revealed? For he shall grow up before him as a tender plant, and as a root out of a dry ground: he hath no form nor comeliness; and when we shall see him, there is no beauty that we should desire him. He is despised and rejected of men; a man of sorrows, and acquainted with grief: and we hid as it were our faces from him; he was despised, and we esteemed him not. Surely he hath borne our griefs, and carried our sorrows: yet we did esteem him stricken, smitten of God, and afflicted. But he was wounded for our transgressions, he was bruised for our iniquities: the chastisement of our peace was upon him; and with his stripes we are healed. All we like sheep have gone astray; we have turned everyone to his own way; and the LORD hath laid on him the iniquity of us all. He was oppressed, and he was afflicted, yet he opened not his mouth: he is brought as a lamb to the slaughter, and as a sheep before her shearers is dumb, so he openeth not his mouth. He was taken from prison and from judgment: and who shall declare his generation? for he was cut off out of the land of the living: for the transgression of my people was he stricken. And he made his grave with the wicked, and with the rich in his death; because he had done no violence, neither was any deceit in his mouth" (Isaiah 53: 1-9).

Figure 13. Despite the thorn-covered calyx, there is a precious and fragrant rose waiting to bloom. Hope is what we cling to as we journey on this side of the universe. Ignore the trials, worry and struggle; concentrate on the blessings bestowed, and life will become more meaningful and interesting (Photograph by author)

Too Hurry... (2015)

"So it's beginning to look a lot like Christmas…"
Holly hanging, bells chiming, mall hopping,
Everyone appears to be smiling; even those who never smiled before…
While all year long we never stop to look…
At the destitute, the poor, who come to our door;
And there she was, sitting on the last treader
In the stairwell I descended,
With hands outstretched begging;
Begging without looking me in the eye,
Hoping that I will drop in her hand a few coins;
Coins that I may never spend,
Yes, her harrowed face stained with worry…her hair unkempt;
Sitting there pleading with the public,
With me, perhaps for a morsel of bread
And I passed; I just passed her as though she did not exist,
I managed a glance, the thought came…
To investigate her need; her sore need,
But I was too hurry; too hurry to care,
And now I jog my mind to the very moment, the very scene…
The nuance that expired at the instance,
My conscience plagues me now like a nasty curse,
Will I ever see her again?
To make up for my error, to give to her of my purse,
Sitting there hoping, probably praying,
For some soul to have mercy,
Sitting there she was; languishing in anguish,
On the step in the stairwell,
How could I be so crass, so callous?
Why so uncaring? Why so inconsiderate?
About someone who was so in need of me,
How do I forgive myself?
Now Christmas is here…great!
And I think of the tree, the decorations…
The carols, the nice food,
The presents…hmmm,
What will she have?
And what do I have to be joyous about?
Will I enjoy Christmas?
Should I rejoice in the celebration of the one who came?
To save us from our sins…From my sins, my lack of conscience,
My lack of love and kindness; for I am so wretched and undone,
Too hurry; O so hurry!
To care,
Do you feel this way sometimes?

Figure 14. The view to the south from The Abbey of Our Lady of Exile. The valley below exhibits the urban sprawl in the city of Tunapuna and environs. In the distance is the Central Range where the highest elevation (308 metres or 1009 feet) is Mount Tamana. (Photograph by author)

Mount Saint Benedict was founded on October 06, 1912 by a small group of monks from the ancient Abbey of San Sebastien in Brazil. These men sought refuge in Trinidad by fleeing the threat of religious persecution. Under the astute leadership of Don Mayeul de Caigny, permission was sought from the Archbishop of Port of Spain, John Pius Dowling, to identify a suitable location in Trinidad. After searching for three months, Don Mayuel was invited to visit an estate located in the mountainous region of Tunapuna and was captivated by the ambience embodying PAX (Peace), the quality all Benedictine monks seek (Rule of Saint Benedict, Prologue vs. 17). The monastery was to be built 600 feet above sea level (asl) and the land was dedicated to the Blessed Virgin Mary under the title of "Our Lady of Exile," as the account from the Gospel of Matthew (Matthew Ch. 2: 13-18) reminded them of their own flight. Due to the tenacity and discipline of the Benedictine monks, the Monastery grew from the humble beginnings of an "ajoupa" to several buildings which included a church, various workshops, accommodation and bakery, indicating the Monastery was here to stay. It soon became an accepted centre of Catholic life and worship in Trinidad. (Information stated here was copied from the signboard up at the abbey)

In Our House (2016)
In our house...We explore the bush...you and me
To fetch a branch for a Christmas tree;
Guava, Black sage, Casuarina...whatever it be,
Covered with cotton wool "snow"...a thing of beauty.

In our house…We scrub and clean, and polish
There's a smell of paint and varnish;
The scent of Christmas greets the air,
The season of joy has come…it's here!

In our house…Fresh new curtains hung all about
"Merry Christmas!" We all will shout;
A day waited for all year long,
Let's come together in a Christmas song!

In our house…Although so poor
We lay new linoleum on the floor;
Renew the bedsheets and pillow cases,
Welcome always, friends with smiling faces.

In our house…The Christ child is lifted high
The Lord our God is always nigh;
Never forget, always remember,
That Jesus came as our precious Savior.

In our house…There's a song in the air,
Sorrel, fruit cake, and ginger beer;
Aroma of cinnamon, sage, rosemary, thyme,
And a turkey soaking in a bucket of brine.

In our house…"Joy to the world the Lord is come!"
His Spirit invited home;
"Come let us adore him,"
Rest awhile from the noisy din.

In our house…There is no fuss,
Come in…sup with us.

The Pilgrimage of the Magi…

"Now when Jesus was born in Bethlehem of Judaea in the days of Herod the king, behold, there came wise men from the east to Jerusalem, Saying, Where is he that is born King of the Jews? for we have seen his star in the east, and are come to worship him. When Herod the king had heard *these things*, he was troubled, and all Jerusalem with him. And when he had gathered all the chief priests and scribes of the people together, he demanded of them where Christ should be born. And they said unto him, In Bethlehem of Judaea: for thus it is written by the prophet, and thou Bethlehem, *in* the land of Juda, art not the least among the princes of Juda: for out of thee shall come a Governor, that shall rule my people Israel. Then Herod, when he had privily called the wise men, inquired of them diligently what time the star appeared. And he sent them to Bethlehem, and said, Go and search diligently for the young child; and when ye have found *him*, bring me word again, that I may come and worship him also. When they had heard the king, they departed; and, lo, the star, which they saw in the east, went before them, till it came and stood over where the young child was"
(Matthew 2:1-11)

Figure 15 …and they brought gold, frankincense, and myrrh. The Savior was born! (Photograph by author)

The Only Hope (2017)

If you have come to the end of your rope,
And you are still holding on…there is hope,
If confusion rises like a storm in your brain,
Know this, the rainbow follows the rain.

With all the stress of the lingering year,
The sun will shine, you should not fear,
For people come, and yes, people also go,
But God is always there—I guess we all know.

For in the straw-lined cradle,
There our Savior lay in the stable,
He came, He lived, He healed, He wept,
A man of sorrows, on the hills of Jerusalem slept.

For without Him there is no peace, no joy, no life!
Mary's baby boy came to end our earthly strife,
The Christmas feelings that fill our hearts,
His to bestow on us, right from the start.

But filled with sorrow and acquainted with grief,
He hung on the cross and said to the thief,
"Today you will be with me in paradise,"
He loved, He forgave, despite His demise.

Many there are who hate His name, His word,
Many there are who seek not the precious Lord,
But I say it now, as I have said before,
His hand of love reaches out to us forevermore.

Yes, at every Christmas we trim the tree,
Set bright presents beneath for you and me,
Remember well as we celebrate His birth,
He bought us back; for a lost world, the only hope.

Figure 16. Made from beaked hazelnut wood and created to represent a tiny cord of wood, I shipped this ornament to be part of the decorations for a Christmas tree in Bachus, Minnesota. (Photograph by Ronald A. Royer, PhD)

...show love to foreigners
"For the Lord your God is the God of gods and Lord of lords. He is the great God, the mighty and awesome God, who shows no partiality and cannot be bribed. He ensures that orphans and widows receive justice. He shows love to the foreigners living among you and gives them food and clothing. So you, too, must show love to foreigners, for you yourselves were once foreigners in the land of Egypt" (Deuteronomy 10:17–19).

The flight to Egypt: "When they saw the star, they rejoiced with exceeding great joy. And when they were come into the house, they saw the young child with Mary his mother, and fell down, and worshipped him: and when they had opened their treasures, they presented unto him gifts; gold, and frankincense, and myrrh. And being warned of God in a dream that they should not return to Herod, they departed into their own country another way. And when they were departed, behold, the angel of the Lord appeareth to Joseph in a dream, saying, Arise, and take the young child and his mother, and flee into Egypt, and be thou there until I bring thee word: for Herod will seek the young child to destroy him. When he arose, he took the young child and his mother by night, and departed into Egypt: And was there until the death of Herod: that it might be fulfilled which was spoken of the Lord by the prophet, saying, Out of Egypt have I called my son" (Matthew 2: 10-11)

Herod slaughters infants: "Then Herod, when he saw that he was mocked of the wise men, was exceeding wroth, and sent forth, and slew all the children that were in Bethlehem, and in all the coasts thereof, from two years old and under, according to the time which he had diligently inquired of the wise men. Then was fulfilled that which was spoken by Jeremy the prophet, saying, In Rama was there a voice heard, lamentation, and weeping, and great mourning, Rachel weeping for her children, and would not be comforted, because they are not" (Matthew 2:16)

The return to Nazareth: "But when Herod was dead, behold, an angel of the Lord appeareth in a dream to Joseph in Egypt, Saying, Arise, and take the young child and his mother, and go into the land of Israel: for they are dead which sought the young child's life. And he arose, and took the young child and his mother, and came into the land of Israel. But when he heard that Archelaus did reign in Judaea in the room of his father Herod, he was afraid to go thither: notwithstanding, being warned of God in a dream, he turned aside into the parts of Galilee: And he came and dwelt in a city called Nazareth: that it might be fulfilled which was spoken by the prophets, He shall be called a Nazarene." (Matthew 2: 19-23)

He that dwelleth in the secret place of the most high shall
abide under the shadow of the Almighty
(Psalm 1: 1)

Christmas Migration (2018)

And there rose a cry!
A cry of sorrow
In Rama was there a voice heard…
For some tiny ones,
No tomorrow!
In Bethlehem…Lamentation,
Weeping, and great mourning,
Rachel weeping for her children,
Rachel cried out in pain…
God have mercy!
In grief…never to be comforted
Her children slaughtered
Streets stained with blood
There was no God!
The children are not

Spoken of Jeremy the prophet…
O the rot!
An emperor so devilish! So rabid!
In the City of David
A madman, full of hate
A lunatic; wroth!
The horror of the sword
And yet the Living Word
Escaped!
On a donkey
In his mother's arms
By night he fled
To another place; a better place
A place secure
A place of providence
To suckle in peace
For he, our Lord
Was not to be murdered
By a power hungry freak
For sure all of us will
Must one day lie still
The monarch faded…gone!
For out of Egypt have I called my son!
And then we turn our gaze
To modern pages
We see children locked in cages
Defenseless, yet hoping
Crying for freedom
By the Rock of Ages.
O the horror…
While "The Lady" weeps in the harbor.

"Prosperity"
"...and he shall be like a tree planted by the rivers of water,
that bringeth forth his fruit in his season; his leaf also shall
not wither; and whatsoever he doeth shall prosper."
(Psalm 1: 3)

Doh Pass Mih House

Ah have ah pardner name Santo
We used tuh parang wherever we go
He does sing ah good Aguinaldo
Why he leave out mih house me eh know?
He used tuh parang by me every Christmas
Parang till fo' day morn
Ah dunno if he wanted some souse
Buh last year he leave out mih house.

Ah know, he parang Sotoro
He went, he sing fuh Rudolpho
By he compie he lime in Lopinot
Why he leave out mih house me eh know?
He know ah living over dey in Pinto,
Ah squatting right dey dong by Locho
No fence, no dog...ah have ah open yard
Tuh parang by me, it eh hard.

Yuh come, yuh pass through Valencia
Yuh pass mih tuh reach tuh Arima
Ah hear yuh went tuh Palo Seco
Why yuh leave out mih house me eh know?
Santo boi ah have dis longing
The lavway with you I must sing
Ah have some pastelle...ah good pot ah souse
O come and parang in mih house.

Ah old, ah feeble, and ah rel poor
Ah piece ah string jus tie up mih door
Right next door yuh parang by Puelto

Then yuh sing over dey by Portillo
Ah know the sound of yuh cuatro
Di one yuh buy from Aparicio
Ah sit dong ah wait till di cock crow
Why yuh leave out mih house just so.

Santo…doh pass mih house, doh pass mih house,
Doh pass mih house when yuh parang
Ah beggin' doh pass mih house, doh pass mih house
Doh pass mih house…bring di gang
Ah beggin' doh pass mih house, doh pass mih house…
Leh we parang on Christmas Eve
Ah go play di "**Bells of St. Mary**,"
Just come and parang by we.

Figure 17. Hanging from an oak tree at Camp Metigoshe, North Dakota, is the finest model of "**The Bells of St. Mary**." Made in Arima, Trinidad, this precious instrument was the personal cuatro of the maker. A little bruised and battered, this cuatro is probably the only one of its kind in existence today…sweet as ever! (Photograph by Ronald A. Royer, PhD)

"The Bells of St. Mary"

Some people hang up their guns, some their shoes. I eventually hung up my old cuatro. Ronald A. Royer (Emeritus Professor of Science), my friend and former mentor, took this picture of my faithful cuatro, "The Bells of St. Mary" hanging from an oak tree in Camp Metigoshe, North Dakota. I bought this cuatro in 1980. While at the camp, I thought that this cuatro needed a rest. Although it still has a sweet and delectable "voice," it is resting peacefully with its scars on top of my bookshelf. I jog my memory to remember the name of the cuatro maker who sold to me this wonderful instrument. All I could recall is that he resided at Alice Street, Arima. It was Christmas week and I sorely needed a cuatro; desperate and hoping to find a reasonably-priced one, I went to the Louis Gilman Thomas music store, way up on Frederick Street, Port of Spain, to purchase an instrument. To my disappointment, all the less expensive cuatros were sold! It was terrifying! My life was now in a tailspin. The ones that remained were too expensive for the small change I had in my pocket. I was left in a state of despair. I couldn't think! Quite melancholic, I started walking back to Independence Square to find passage back to Sangre Grande. Dejectedly, I began walking to the taxi stand. Somehow a little "birdie" told me to go over to the Janouras clothing store on Queen Street and have a chat with Paul Castillo, one of the founders of the Trinidad and Tobago Parang Association.

Paul worked there as a store clerk in the gents department. I explained to Paul my situation; my dilemma. I reminded him that once-upon-a-time he came to our tiny house on Adventist Street with some paranderos from Rio Claro…and yes, he remembered. I hastened to relate that the parang that night was one of the best I ever heard! He then directed me to go to Alice Street, Arima where I would meet the cuatro maker who made "The Bells of St. Mary." Not boasting too much, Paul implied that this cuatro maker made the sweetest sounding cuatros in Trinidad and Tobago. Without reservation, Paul lauded the work of this wonderful artisan. I hastened to reach to Alice Street. When I arrived, the aging cuatro maker wearing a weather-beaten felt hat, greeted me at the door. I told him what I came for and he invited me in. His wife also greeted me and offered me a seat next to her dining table. They were so kind and gentle…two really beautiful people.

Without hesitation the man told me that he had no more cuatros for sale but showed to me his very own cuatro. I asked him if he would sell me this precious instrument. The expression on his face revealed to me that he did not want to part with this instrument. He said that it was his personal cuatro and that it was not for sale. My heart sank. I pulled out the $180 I had in my wallet and made an offer for the instrument. I really "coveted" the instrument. He looked at me and shook his head…and that shake meant "nah." Nevertheless, unbeknownst to me, his wife was in my corner. She said: "Gih di boi the cuatro nah…yuh doh even play it anymore." I blurted out "Yes!" I instantly reminded him that he could always make one for himself. It seemed that he was not going to crack. This was a special cuatro! The back of the instrument was not made of cedar as all the other cuatros I had played. The back of this one was made with a different type of wood. I asked him, "Mango wood?" "Lipinet?" he just smiled.

One hundred and eighty dollars was quite a sum of money to pass up in those days. He played a few notes on it for me, and oh what a tone and resonance. He saw in my eyes how desperate I was. Then he handed the cuatro to me. I started to play and didn't want to stop. He was so impressed that he said, "Okay son, you win! You can have the cuatro." Could you imagine the joy I felt?

I own two more cuatros, "Sonah," and "Vega de Oropouche," they are good sounding ones, but every time I look at "The Bells of St. Mary," I remember the first time I played that sweet and delightful Trini made instrument. I probably had the only cuatro left that was made by this great luthier who lived on Alice Street, Arima. Yes, The Bells of Saint Mary passed through a few mishaps, even to the point where I almost lost it. It fell and was broken at one time. A cuatro maker whom I knew only by the name "Couzin" from Palo Seco, Trinidad, repaired the damage. Then there was another incident when it was broken down the side. I almost died when this happened. Nevertheless, I repaired the damage and The Bells of Saint Mary is still alive! The "Bells of Saint Mary" is now lodged at Simon Music Supplies, located at 20 Borde Street, Port od Spain, Trinidad.

A story about "The Little Pink House & Christmas"

As I sat on the back stairs of my apartment, memories of my childhood chased each other in my mind until I decided to write about *The Little Pink House*. In this adobe abode, Christmas was like living in a fairy tale. During that early era of my life while I resided in that house, all I could do was dream. And here I was in North Dakota, practically homesick as I thought about my childhood while I watched the geese fly by with their intermittent honking.

As if it were just yesterday, I remember the night we migrated from Picton Street to the corner of Adventist and Ramdass Streets, Sangre Grande to *The Little Pink House*. I will never forget the muddy track and the steady hand of my aging Aunt Emelda holding on to my tiny hand while we ambled through the darkness, roughly sixty years ago. Although the swampy area is famous for the deadly coral snake, barefooted with a little bundle in hand, I trudged along close to my aunt. I had no idea where we were going but I trusted my good aunty "Melda." She was such a blessed woman.

The next seven years living with my eight siblings and an overworked mom were quite eventful, not to mention the heated sibling rivalry on occasion. It was during this period I was baptized in the crystal waters of the Valencia River that flowed just beyond the World War II American checkpoint pillars on the Eastern Main Road, Valencia. On that Sunday morning, the water was clear and cold, which reminded me that I would now be able to see things a little clearer in a cold and sometimes unfriendly world.

Despite my internal struggles, I have not stopped attending *church*. As a matter of fact, I attend *any* church in view because no religion is perfect…of course, we all know that righteousness precedes religion. I do not worship at the shrine of religion. Once it enhances my educational development, I glean wisdom from every *point* of the compass. My successful completion of the Common Entrance Examination (CE) and departure from the elementary school stage was a milestone. I became a collegiate at Northeastern College, Sangre Grande, Trinidad, and it was there that I read for the Cambridge University, General Certificate Examinations.

Life in secondary school was a trial by fire; it was survival of the fittest. Coping with studies in, biology, art, mathematics, physics, agricultural science, health science, English language, chemistry, and woodwork without some of my personal textbooks was more than enough to bear. Sometimes I didn't know how I made it through the day. Compounding the myriad problems I suffered at this school were some of the "teachers" who did nothing more than to ridicule, insult, and embarrass me with their sarcasm and innuendo. Yes they did! I remember! Why? I guess they too had their problems that they lugged to school each day. Maybe I was a student that they did not fancy. Was it the way I looked, my clothes, my shoes, my religion, my reactions? Who knows? I was a poor, fatherless and struggling student. Despite the ills and difficulties at school, I came home to *The Little Pink House* where I would sit on the wooden back steps and reshape my own world.

My mother was untiring in her effort to provide palatable food and clean clothes for us. I remember the coconut bake (flatbread) and scrambled egg sandwiches, guava jam and peanut butter, saltfish (cod) buljol and "blue food" (dasheen—*Colocasia esculenta*), the yam and moko, fried fish, callaloo and stewed common (yard) fowl, the split peas and dumplings and yes, ochro rice "cook up" with coconut milk and salted beef. Good food I say, but nothing came near to the taste of my mother's sancoche, nothing! Her sancoche was a boil up of split peas or pigeon peas with dasheen, green bananas, yam, eddoes, and salted pigtail, salted beef, or salted codfish. Sometimes she would add some dasheen leaves and coconut milk to add more flavor to the pot. I did not like split peas and rice cookup with salt fish… but I ate it anyway.

I sold newspapers, beer and rum bottles I found on the roadside, worked in a lime (citrus) field in the summer, cleaned people's yards, made and sold bamboo brooms, and did whatever could have earned a penny or two to help with the family income and buy some of my school books. And yes, I studied. I read everything in sight when we had electricity and when we used candles. We used candles when we could not have paid the electricity bills. I was hungry for knowledge, yearning to succeed. Such was the life in *The Little Pink House*, but it was part of the dream becoming a reality. Christmas time was the best part though in *The Little Pink House* in that blessed corner. It was as though a special light shone on that *Little Pink House* where a single mom and her nine children dwelt. Those times were hard economic times, "Guava season"—hard times, after my father deserted us. Up to this day no one knows why he left and I do not care to know, for the memory of the infidel is forgotten, as one who is dead without a gravestone marker. My older brothers and sisters really cared for us smaller ones and tried to make us happy with whatever they could have provided.

Long gone are the days when we used to find fun in *leepaying* [plastering… covering made with cow dung and dirt (from Bhojpuri Hindustani)] the house. The house was made of *tapia* (adobe) and every year we would mix cow's dung (gobar), tapia grass, and clay to patch the holes in the house just before Christmas. It was great fun to pelt the remnants of the plaster at each other and then go take a standpipe spray down. When the plasterwork dried we would mix whitewash and red ochre to get the right tone of pink for *The Little Pink House*. Windows, doors and sills were painted in brown or green. *The Little Pink House* glowed. The lawn was brush cut with a *swiper* (brushing cutlass; langmat or boze) and the walkway edged to perfection. Muddy box drains around were cleaned and even the path to the pit latrine was clinically groomed. Although we had no idea where Christmas presents and food were coming from, everything was done to welcome Christmas.

Good people are everywhere; Christmas brings them out of the woodwork. Without fail, the toys and the food came from somewhere…only God knows. Maybe there is a Santa Claus. I remember I saw a pair of plastic binoculars in the toy store that I really wanted. It was priced for just about TT$1.50 (US$0.25). I prayed and prayed and prayed for this simple little toy. What a dreamer I was, but was overjoyed to find it under the guava branch Christmas tree on Christmas morning. I could still remember the smell of hot homemade bread, coconut sweet bread and black fruitcake in the house on Christmas morning. And yes, the bright red sorrel drink brewed from the flowers of the sorrel plant (*Hibiscus sabdariffa*) and that *infernal* ginger beer that I used to dislike because it burned my throat on its way down. Memories, memories, memories.

The joy and wonder of Christmas was told in the *Parang* (Parranda). How lovely it was to get out of bed at two o'clock in the morning to welcome a group of *paranderos* singing a sweet Spanish "serena" (troubadour poetic or musical composition that used to be sung at night) outside the front door. Happiness, peace and joy was the language the music spoke. It was all about the annunciation of

Angel Gabriel to the Virgin Mary and the miracle of salvation. Sometimes the singers were old men with missing teeth but the melody sounded even sweeter with the accompaniment of a good *cuatro*, mandolin, saltbox base, *toc-toc* and a *shac-shac* (maracas). And oh yes, the coffee pot would be on the stove, and *sancoche* and sweetbread would be served; we shared whatever we had with the paranderos. I remember Paul Castillo one of the founders of *The Trinidad and Tobago Parang Association* and Jules Riley with his band of *paranderos* from Rio Claro coming to our house. Our house always received a special blessing at Christmas. We had so little, yet we gave so much…the love, the cheer, the joy that we experienced because we were contented with what we had. It did not matter if we hung plastic "curtains," it did not matter if we did not have new clothes; it did not matter if people poked fun at us. All that mattered was the fact that that we knew Christ, His great and matchless love and how we kept him in our hearts in *The Little Pink House*. Sometimes I wish for some of those moments we shared in that house…so distant now.

Figure 18. A beautiful quaint rural landscape in Tobago. Think of all the Christmas cards mailed from the red mailbox and all the Christmas greeting calls made from the phonebooth (Photograph by author)

Unless…

Unless we seek to rid the "me" inside of me,
Enable the mastery of humility,
To stifle the pig, the brute,
That shackles the truth,
Unless…

Unless we supplant ritual, liturgy, and dogma,
Defy the sophistries of the mind bender,

Dismantle the tunnel where people grovel,
To find the light, to know that no religion is right,
Unless…

Unless we mortify the beasts!
Blood-sucking demons wallowing in a greedy feast,
Supporters of underground sweatshops…child slavery,
Those enemies of humanity,
Unless…

Unless we see each other as family; as equals,
To help with a kind lift if another falls,
For whatever the reason,
Some may not be as fortunate in any season,
Unless…

Unless we see heart muscle with common color,
Unless we see not lighter skin pigment as one superior,
Unless we see our neighbor as sister, as brother,
Unless we see the *ant* as teacher,
Unless…

The Network of Souls

Whether we want to believe it or not, we are *family*. All of us are connected! Isn't it interesting that we are all related? Despite the truth, some would continue to argue about who is better than whom. We were born on the Earth, and note carefully, all of us are born *of* the Earth. We were not born elsewhere. We came from the same dirt, the same mud and mire; the same clay in which plants grow and produce food to sustain life.

Everything we possess or think that we "own" came from the Earth. The Earth provides sustenance and feeds all of us. Some people, from whence they emerged, may possess more "things," more food, more water, and more privileges. That does not mean that anyone is better or worse than the person next door because we are all connected in some form or the other. Do we not all breathe the same air? Can you determine or identify which molecule of oxygen you will breathe in today or tomorrow?

Connectivity, abstract as it may seem, accommodates all directions. Some of us do not recognize this aspect of life. In view of this *connectivity*, plants are connected with all of us, even deeper than we think. However, we become disconnected when we see or visualize a community as "we" and "them." Yes, when we ignore the plurality; yes, the mind-boggling variety and diversity in nature.

In the photograph, I saw connectivity and connections…branches and twigs intersecting, reaching out, stretching to embrace each other. In the silence of that moment I could hear them saying, "We are one! Let us form this canopy." I saw *interdependence* a spiritual sharing, unsurpassed. The branches said, "Let us spread the love…let us glorify our creator." The branches literally danced before me in praise!

'Twas an example, as though nature wanted to make a sterling announcement to me about the world in which we live.

Figure 19. While sitting on a park bench in Harris Square, Port of Spain, I managed to look up into the tree under which I sat. This is what I saw. Something special is going on here. "Do you see you what I see?" This is one of my favorite photographs (Photograph by author)

In that brief but inspirational moment, it was clear that despite the struggle, we as humans should live in peace and harmony. As the branches were interwoven, I surmised that we are all different, but not at all deficient. Some of the branches looked tough and gnarly, so indicative of the battle we all have for light, food and acceptance. The branches, as well as the twigs on the periphery, had a role to play; they all factored! They all had a place! All contributed to make up the whole; a canopy so refreshingly beautiful.

This immaculate view transmitted to my mentality that no one is useless; no one is dysfunctional or deformed; some just prefer to take another route, another road, another avenue, another direction. Each branch took the opportunity to explore its very own potential, its own environment, its very own style and appreciation of space.

Nonetheless, each branch was committed to the task; the formation of a *network*, full of art and music; the beauty and essence of life. Such a lesson book of wisdom! They believed in each other. They agreed with each other. They entertained each other. What a *holy* and wonderful orchestration of unity and purpose! And so should we in this human *network of souls* must harmonize, must reach out to each other, must make *music* together. Just as the branches and twigs of this canopy, we must work together, we must synchronize with synergy to shape a better place, to form a better union, to establish a position of equality for all; to establish a better life with overflowing bushels of hope for all. Could we begin this Christmas?

A Christmas of Nothing

In almost everyone's experience, there are times when they are up, and there are times when they're down. Christmas is a time for enjoyment, but when there's nothing with which to celebrate, the joy diminishes like a dying sun in the west. Well, there was a year when our house was "dry," but hope for a Christmas blessing was always high. Poverty got the better of us. Food was scarce and there was always a struggle to meet the monthly payment for rent.

Around that time, I was attending Northeastern College (NEC) and part of my education at school included Agricultural Science. Note well, at NEC, I was very astute regarding my attention to the subject of agricultural science. I somehow knew that if I understood how to grow food that I would never be hungry. I loved the land, the two-acre plot where we cultivated a variety of crops. I spent most of my "free time" looking after what I planted there. As part of the practicum, the school involved the few agriculture students in the raising of broiler chickens. I found myself quite engaged in the preparation of the site for the chicken coop. When it was time to erect the building I was chief cook and bottle washer until we spread the "bagasse" (chicken litter) for the arrival of day-old chicks. I cannot remember how many chicks we introduced to the coop, maybe 200. Nevertheless, we were given the routine to tend the chickens for eight weeks during the Christmas term.

Needless to say, our house promised literally nothing for Christmas. Christmas was around the corner and there was no joy and gladness in sight. There was a somber atmosphere of despair and hopelessness. Many factors contributed to our demise of which I will make no mention. Despite our efforts to plant a kitchen garden which we hoped would have supplemented part of our diet. Sad to say, the kitchen garden was fraught with failures. Nature wasn't so kind to us that year. The few roots of cassava became infested with a worm that destroyed the apical buds of the plants causing the yields to be quite small. The *bodi* (asparagus or snake bean) did not produce as expected, but we had ochro in abundance. Stretching from the road to the end of the allotment, the line of ochro trees went crazy with their production! During this time of food scarcity, we ate whatever cassava roots we could have harvested. Almost all of the roots were small, lean, and tiny, but we managed. Complementing the cassava, almost every day, we had boiled common fowl (yard fowl) eggs, a few bodi, and boiled ochro seasoned with salt, black pepper and cooking oil. We followed my mother's mantra, "Eat little and live long." She also said to us: "If you don't want it. Sit down by it." We had to make do with what we had.

Some of the ochro remained and dried on the trees. We collected almost five pounds of dried seeds during that season. Wondering what to do with the dried seeds, someone from the church we attended told my mother to parch (roast) the seeds in a pot and grind them to make a kind of *postum* for us to drink. She did as she was told, and to our surprise, the postum was quite refreshing and tasty. I will never forget the ventures of my mother to provide food for us. In the "ochro seed story," almost the whole class at the Eastern Caribbean Institute for Agriculture and Forestry (ECIAF) laughed at me when I told them about "Ochro Tea." The lecturer concerned with vegetable production was talking about ochro production and asked us what we think are the uses of ochro. Everyone knew that ochro is used primarily in the preparation of "Crab and Callaloo," the national dish of in Trinidad and Tobago, and most people know about ochro "choka;" chopped ochro fried up with onions, garlic, and chili pepper. This choka is normally eaten with saada roti, a flatbread made with bleached or whole wheat flour, salt, and baking powder. No one ever heard about "Ochro Tea." In the wake of this new information and ensuing laughter, I was labeled with the nickname "Ochro Tea," at least for a couple of weeks.

Returning to my experiences at school, Christmas week came with the receipt of two huge broiler chickens, at least seven or eight pounds each. They were nice healthy birds. My mother was overjoyed with the fact that at least we were having chicken for Christmas. But that was not all. The day before Christmas eve, after having received permission from Mr. Kelvin Branche, my Agricultural Science teacher (A teacher I will never forget!), I went up to the school garden to see what I could have found to bring home for Christmas.

To my surprise, the dwarf pigeon pea (*Cajanus cajan*) trees were in full fruit. Pea seeds were planted about three months before. I harvested about ten pounds of full pods. That was not all. There was another surprise. Some stray sweet potato vines that we *rogued* from the garden were thrown upon a heap of well-rotted bagasse and vegetable material, literally a compost heap. The vines took root. I noticed that the vines looked a bit shabby and dry so I ventured to investigate why. Lo and behold, about 18 inches deep in the middle of the compost heap was a nest of what to me looked like huge smooth round eggs, light pink in color. I became sort of "frightened" for a moment until I realized that the extremely fertile conditions of the compost had created the optimum conditions for the production of sweet potato. This red colored potato was the variety known as "O49," a variety developed by the University of the West Indies (UWI). I removed close to twenty pounds of potato. The school's garden provided all we needed to celebrate Christmas…and we were thankful.

I remembered quite well the maxim: "Man's extremity is God's opportunity." Always keep hope alive. What seemed in the beginning to be a drab and dull Christmas; a Christmas of nothing, became a Christmas full of joy, glad tidings and food for all. We will never forget…never!

Light Notes

- *Grope not towards the light at the end of the tunnel but rather remove the tunnel and stand in the light.*
- *Light is there for all, those with sight; even the blind, but seeing the light depends on one thing, the opening of the eye.*
- *The way we position ourselves in the world will determine how much light we reflect, and how much warmth we will feel.*
- *What you can see in the day, wait not till night to take a candle to find.*
- *Light caution…the devil can transform himself into an angel of light.*
- *No one could appreciate what is truly light without first acknowledging what is truly darkness.*
- *There is a moment between light and darkness that we tend not to decipher or is it that we choose not to?*
- *Knowing about the light is one thing, but knowing "The Light" is best.*
- *Finding light is not difficult; follow your spirit.*

Figure 20. A precious candle glowing in the night on the fence of the Cordettes Steelpan yard, Foster Road, Sangre Grande. Trinidad. It was a candle lit for Ken "Professor" Philmore, a steelpan icon of great and noble repute who went on his way to the "Panyard of Glory." May the "Light & Truth" that this candle represents, remain etched in our hearts as we celebrate peace and joy with all at every Christmas and more importantly, the love we give to each other every day of the year! (Photograph by author)

MERRY CHRISTMAS!

Printed in the United States
By Bookmasters